The Secret Of Abundance And The

Art Of Getting Rich

L. W. de Laurence

Kessinger Publishing's Rare Reprints

Thousands of Scarce and Hard-to-Find Books on These and other Subjects!

- Americana
- Ancient Mysteries
- Animals
- Anthropology
- Architecture
- Arts
- Astrology
- Bibliographies
- Biographies & Memoirs
- Body, Mind & Spirit
- Business & Investing
- Children & Young Adult
- Collectibles
- Comparative Religions
- Crafts & Hobbies
- Earth Sciences
- Education
- Ephemera
- Fiction
- Folklore
- Geography
- Health & Diet
- History
- Hobbies & Leisure
- Humor
- Illustrated Books
- Language & Culture
- Law
- Life Sciences

- Literature
- Medicine & Pharmacy
- Metaphysical
- Music
- Mystery & Crime
- Mythology
- Natural History
- Outdoor & Nature
- Philosophy
- Poetry
- Political Science
- Science
- Psychiatry & Psychology
- Reference
- Religion & Spiritualism
- Rhetoric
- Sacred Books
- Science Fiction
- Science & Technology
- Self-Help
- Social Sciences
- Symbolism
- Theatre & Drama
- Theology
- Travel & Explorations
- War & Military
- Women
- Yoga
- *Plus Much More!*

**We kindly invite you to view our catalog list at:
http://www.kessinger.net**

The Master Key

CHAPTER XXXVI.

LESSON THIRTY-FOUR.

THE SECRET OF ABUNDANCE.

THE POVERTY CURE.

Poverty is as much a disease as pleurisy, only the former attacks the *mind* and the latter the *body*. You never knew an energetic, spirited and pushing man really poor. The poor in purse are almost invariably poor in mind. Of course, one must not include in this category people who prefer leading a simple existence, with no hankering after servants, motor cars, large establishments and a thousand-and-one et ceteras which characterize modern life. There are many who, with a humble cottage and plain fare, scarcely have any use for money, their wants being so few. By poverty I mean a state in which men can scarcely get enough to eat or cannot pay their way as they would like. Going a step higher, I should include among those whose ambitions rise above their means—but I am not concerned at present with this class. My present aim is to stimulate those who are in want of means to sustain life comfortably; to show them a way out; to revive that hope which once they had in abundance, but which contact with the world has well-nigh utterly obliterated.

The cure of poverty, it must be admitted at the outset, is no light task, but it is curable in nearly every case. It does not seem to have occurred to people (except a very few) that no one need be poor. The saying about the poor being always with us seems to have been taken as an utterance that applied to all countries and ages, and the problem of the unemployed, which every civilized nation has to face, lends color to the idea. As a matter of fact if we take Nature we see that she is almost wantonly extravagant. Look at the millions of seeds produced in flowers which cannot possibly grow up. Note the myriads of tiny cells which constitute the spawn of fish; mark the lavishness and prodigality with which vegetation covers our fair earth, and you will recognize that there is nothing miserly or stinting about Dame Nature. This is really a lesson for man, if he could but see it in the right light, and I, like many writers on the subjects of *faith and confidence in one's self,* have been endeavoring to the best of my powers to scatter broadcast during the last few years the conception that no intelligent, able human being need be in dire want.

One of the objections frequently raised by those opposed to a sensible socialism (not the view put forward today by socialists) is that there is not enough money to go round, and it has been affirmed that the earth could not produce sufficient food to maintain the inhabitants if the number grew beyond a certain proportion. These good people forget that not a tithe of the treasures of the earth have been extracted, and that science would have to be reckoned with where the question of food supply was concerned. I merely instance this objection because it stands in the way of reform with many people.

First, the well-fed moneyed class consider that the state of things is irremediable, and then the poor man imagines that conditions as we know them today are part of the natural order of things, and that if he were not in poverty somebody else would be, and that it might as well, perhaps, be himself who should suffer, and so he loses whatever grit he has in him, and he becomes what many would be inclined to call "philosophic," but which I should prefer to designate "resigned."

I trust I have effectually removed this barrier, and now comes another and important one which bars the way to plenty—the *belief* that the ability to make money is only given to a few people who are really clever; or that there are a class of people who may be termed *"lucky."* I think I have shown in this volume that there is no such thing as luck or chance. We must admit that people differ mentally as well as physically, but it is frequently more in degree than in kind, and it is often the case with those who have had a defective bringing up or a scanty education that they are prone to exaggerate their weaknesses. This exaggeration acts very prejudicially, and is at the root of much of the poverty amongst the people.

To cure poverty you *must believe* what is an absolute fact —*that you are of use in some way;* that you have something in you, that the impression of your acquaintances that you are a very commonplace person is merely an impression *caused* by your own conduct. In turn this impression has re-acted on you till you begin to believe firmly where before you had only a suspicion. It will show in your conversation, stamp itself in your walk, your features, your manner all round. You advertise your littleness wherever you go by your appearance, and servility clinches the unfavorable opinion formed of you by a prospective employer.

All that is written above should be read and re-read till it *burns* into the mind as the cure of poverty has been revealed.

To get a better opinion of yourself *think*. I know it is the most difficult task that could be set all poor folk. Had they learned to think they would not have been poor. They would rather do anything than think. Many will plead that they are not cut out for thinking;—they have had no education— *Shakespeare* hadn't, but it did not prevent his becoming a genius. Few self-made men have had any education, and many men highly educated are as poor as crows. We live in the busiest age on record, and the hands or brain of every human being are urgently needed. If you went to an employer of labor and told him you had an idea which would save his expenses by a third, or increase the efficiency of his business, do you suppose you would not gain his ear, if you approached him in the right attitude? Improvements are capable of being made in everything you can mention. Once you have learned to *concentrate* your mind and *think* you have solved the problem of poverty, and for this reason: You have opened up unsuspected avenues of thought, suggestions that will mean money to you in the long run. You have the same stuff in you as *Milton, Goethe, Edison,* but it never occurred to you, did it? It only wants rousing, bringing into activity. Every man is a gold mine to himself, and instead of letting others exploit him he should exploit himself.

It is never too late to begin, unless you've turned eighty, and with some men this age would not be an insurmountable barrier.

With a better opinion of yourself and the habit of thinking and controlling your thoughts so as to concentrate them you will begin to make plans; judgment and tact—that rare virtue—will show themselves; means will come to you to overcome difficulties and you will come into possession of that priceless gem—*initiative.* You will see the necessity of being thorough in whatever calling you may take up, so that an employer can *rely* upon you. Once gain the confidence of an employer and poverty and you will rarely meet. Make it a point to know your business from top to bottom; concentrate your mind on your duties willingly, with a light heart, for you are building for the future.

Get into close touch with the very poor and you will find that they invariably consider that only people with *marked* ability can *"get on."* You can have ability just as well as any one else. It is not the prerogative of kings; the poorest and humblest man may cultivate it, but, mark well, *thinking* is the basis of it, for by it you dispel ignorance, the greatest curse from which mankind suffers today. Willingness to learn is a sign of the successful man, and as ability is gained the other dread ally of Poverty—*Fear*—(they always go together, therefore by destroying the one you destroy both) will loosen its hold of your heart-strings, and hope will take up its abode.

At this point you should take stock of yourself. You will now have valuable assets, and the next step is to make the most of them. Are you working with system? Are you utilizing your time well? Are you getting the best and highest out of yourself? Do not be content till you do. Whatever plan you may have commenced give it a fair trial. Too many cases of failure have arisen from giving up too soon and not sticking with bulldog tenacity. To the man who sets his teeth and vows he will go through, whatever the cost Fate, gives way.

It is a well-known fact in psychology that an idea, even though devoid of truth, a mere delusion, if held sufficiently long in mind, becomes at length to be regarded as a truth. A knowledge of this law is of incalculable worth to you. Test it now if you are poor. Apply it to your own case. *Banish* for the time being the canker of care, the paralyzing effect of worry and doubt in yourself. Probably you have been indulging in the luxury of these mental visitors for days or weeks, so you can afford to dispense with them for ten or twenty minutes. I know full well the great sacrifice I am asking you to make, for you have an idea that by turning over these worries separately you are deriving a species of sympathy which is very comforting. You have, perhaps, poured your woes into the ears of friends, some willing and others the reverse. You have afforded the only solace that life holds out, just as some people are only happy when they are miserable. When you are miserable the state is *so infectious* that your friends avoid you when circumstances permit.

We are all familiar with the class of persons who are always finding fault and picking holes or criticising others or things generally, deriving immense satisfaction and comfort from the discomfort they cause. Probably they have seen no harm in this habit of supplying sympathy to themselves. As a matter of fact, their greatest enemy could not have inflicted a greater injury upon them. What practical good has it done them? Has the habit solved their problem? What it has done in reality is to have weakened their make-up to an incredible extent; it has literally poisoned the spring of Success. It has magnified their weakness, and their want of self-reliance. Every time you sympathize with a weakness you strengthen that weakness, and render yourself less capable. You paralyze sources of action, destroy initiative, prevent the inception of new ideas, and clog the mental machinery, the one factor which is to *lift you out* of the slough of poverty. It deepens within you the feeling that you are hardly dealt with, that other folk are helped and are "lucky," while everything goes wrong with *you*—I know the feeling, which is better understood than expressed. Get among the unemployed and they will tell you how by a bad trick another fellow *"did them out of a job,"* or how a chap who can't do his work a patch as well as you can has been in regular work for years. Cease whining, cease envying. The men who have kept their places have had some qualifications, for there is not much room for sentiment and favoritism in business. The man who holds a post because he is *"in"* with the foreman, or an official, is on very insecure ground, for changes are frequent, and removal of the foreman may be followed by the dismissal of the incompetent employee. If he does hold his position, however, it is no affair of the other fellow. Every man is concerned with himself alone. It is his business to see that *he* is thoroughly efficient in whatever his calling may be, quick, diligent, reliable, ready to be shown or to learn. Such a man is *certain* of regular employment; he can employ himself, in fact, for as soon as a man has confidence in himself he is fit to be his own employer.

Each time an unkind, mean, angry thought passes through your brain, each time you criticise others, pass judgment on them, discuss their failings with others you are nursing the poverty habit, and for this reason: Poverty is a condition of inharmony; prosperity is a condition of harmony; all criticism, etc., creates inharmony, and it and harmony cannot exist in the mind at the same time. One inevitably neutralizes the other; inharmony antagonizes, and the antagonism being destructive in its character mental force, which is only generated in sufficient quantity to meet the demands made upon it by the body and mind, is *wasted*. This waste of energy might be turned into another channel and produce force which would enable problems to be solved and ideas carried to completion.

Further than this the entertaining of such thoughts cause physical changes in cell tissue, manufacturing by some of those marvellous processes of chemistry poisons which break down the health, and no one who is poor can afford to dispense with good health.

Men who are in poverty and rags do not trust themselves or they would never have been in poverty. They have placed their trust in other people, hoping that *they* would make it all right. If they did not, then fear rushed in, and away went their hope, followed in hot pursuit by self-respect. I do not care how low down a man may be, where he may be placed, however sordid, however apparently hopeless his position, he can remedy it; but the cure must begin by trusting in himself. He has the same force, the same powers at the back of his mind, as all of us. All that is needed is to use them, and a thing can only be used by bringing it into the daily life. By idealizing surroundings and the daily life as outlined above you are insensibly led *away* from poverty and its inevitable degrading surroundings. An actual *"new life"* is lived, and in casting off the influences of the old the mind takes on new aspects— *hope and trust* are born into the nature, and ambition and determination are not far behind.

There will be the belief that circumstances are beginning to change. Poverty and doubt pulls down; hope raises. No one wants to engage a man soddened with the quality of misery or pennilessness; it would "get on the nerves" of many an employer, and when the staff was reduced the man stamped with these qualities would be the first to go.

A man of this type never does good work; he has no "heart," therefore his work is more or less mechanical, and this is soon noticed. We cannot expect employers to be philanthropists. Often they are driven on by the scourge of competition, and cannot help themselves. A bright face is often quite as much a tonic to them as it is to others, and brightness often goes hand-in-hand with intelligence and interest in one's work. A bright disposition often brings about an alert state of mind, frequently leading to keener observation, and inventions are frequently made by workmen of this type. Bright intelligence also often leads to smartness of movement, dexterity in one's calling, and the quick eye of the employer, who is always surrounded by the *"clock-watchers"* and *"stallers,"* soon detects the stuff a man is made of. When an employee really begins to take an interest in his work then he is on the right path.

But it does not necessarily follow that a man in poverty need be an employee. If he will faithfully follow the instructions given in this volume he may devise means by which he will free himself from his cramping environment. Not a quarter of the inventions possible have been invented, not a tithe of the riches in the earth has been suspected, not a thousandth part of the possibilities of existence has been touched up to the present, and all these possibilities are open to *you!* But you must think! When an idea comes along do not dismiss it as wild and improbable, but try and make it as clear as you would the idea of a house you would like to live in. When *Professor Morse* offered to sell his telegraph apparatus to the *American Government* in 1845 for a hundred thousand dollars the offer was refused. Today the *Morse* system is capitalized for two hundred and twenty-two million dollars.

"Professor Alexander Graham Bell offered to sell his telephone patents to the *Western Union Telegraph Co.* for $60,-000, but the officers of the company said it was only a toy and had no commercial value. This same toy, according to the annual report of the *American Telephone and Telegraph Co.,* just issued, earned $160,000,000 last year and has now more than 5,000,000 telephones in use throughout this country."

Of course, I do not imagine that you will initiate a colossal scheme like the first two, although any man, who is not a congenital idiot, may become a genius if he wish. But this illustrates the idea I am endeavoring to make plain—that provided we are fair to ourselves and try to develop more of what is in us we are *certain* to enlarge our mind, or expand our consciousness. Many and many a man fails to improve his surroundings through lightly casting aside an idea which only needed a little more maturing, a little more hatching, to blossom into a really good thing.

It is not education we lack—we have too much of what goes under that name, and the fact that the vast majority of wealthy men were *never conspicuous for their learning* enforces the assertion, but a lifting or a shifting of our conception, a different standard of value of ourselves, and once that different attitude towards ourselves is adopted the way is comparatively smooth.

A hint may be gleaned from the case cited above: *don't get in a rut.* All poverty-stricken men travel in them.

Don't do a thing in the way your forefathers did it, if it can be done in a better manner. Always be on the lookout for improvements, and cultivate the habit of observation. A *Russian* proverb says, *"He goes through the forest and sees no firewood."* By the cultivation of *concentration* and *observation* the wits will be sharpened, and the mind more alert, quick to take advantage of an opportunity, quick to apprehend, and the best aid to that indispensable qualification to all success—executive ability.

Cut yourself off from your newspapers for a time; that is, unless you can discriminate. There is a large number of daily newspapers published in this country, Sunday papers, some of them, printed on cheap paper, and news to match. Analyze any of them and it will be seen that they consist for the greater part of full reports of every crime committed in the United States, and the bulk of the cases occurring in other parts of the world. The most sordid details, the most abject, pitiful, sickening and disgusting items are given as fully as the law of the land will permit. The shady, poverty-sodden side of humanity, with all its weaknesses, its vices, its wickedness, its meanness, craftiness is set forth with such a superabundance of minuteness that not only could a criminal career be learned by it, but it would even induce many weak-minded people to emulate the men figuring in them. Revolting incidents from the divorce court, the hashing up of trickery and chicanery of the world—in a word anything and everything which will not only depress, but will drag the mind down, are to be found in the wretched specimens of the gutter-press. Wallowing in the filth is it any wonder that a man's tastes become debauched, that he loses an interest in good literature, or that he keeps his poverty chains about him?

Never mind being out of date with your news for a few weeks or months. When a crab is going to cast its shell it hides in a crevice where it can lie undisturbed until the new shell has taken the place of the old one, when it can once more go forth. So with a man who would cast off his old mind. While the shedding process is going on let him feed his mind with the best food obtainable—good literature is plentiful and cheap enough, in all conscience. But I would advocate dispensing with cheap newspapers in the ordinary sense, or read only the best with comments on the world's happenings or thoughts. The daily paper has got to be looked upon as a sort of necessity by some people, and it is a good sign when it proceeds from a keen interest in one's country, or progress of mankind, but even this can stand aside for a short time, as can the religious press for much the same reason—they all tend to weaken the optimistic faculty in man. Naturally man is a bundle of hopes, but as one after another is damped by wet blankets hope begins to give up, and then indifference, misery, and finally hopelessness sets in, from which the grave kindly rescues many.

The sensational, and sentimental drama, and sickly poetry are two other sources which contribute to this weakening process. They hold before the eye with dramatic force the conflicting emotions which surge in the human breast, its passions, its foibles, as well as its noblest impulses, and while it may be a veritable mirror of life it is not what many would have. It is a fresh probing of wounds some souls would fain heal, an awakening of sad memories they would prefer to bury forever; an ever-recurring reminder of the dark side of existence, which they would cast from them forever. When we read heart-rending accounts of misery, see plays poignant with grief, we discuss them with friends, or, if we keep silent respecting them, some one will discuss them with us, so that we keep alive within us and sear into our very soul the pains from which we have struggled to free ourselves.

In conclusion, the cure of poverty is the result of real growth, mental and emotional. The nature which is poor in love, in sympathy, in goodwill, belief in himself and his inherent powers is poor in pocket. To stint and stunt the nature is to stint and stunt the money-making possibilities. If you feed on poverty thoughts there is no use for money; it could not be appreciated, and however much might be obtained it would do no good, but would dwindle away.

Many are familiar with the old saw: *"A fool and his money are soon parted."* Most of us have known cases where very poor people, accustomed to live from hand to mouth, having come into money, have soon been in the same plight. The proper use of money can only come to those who have evolved to a point where they can use it intelligently. *Money can never make brains in a man, but brains can make money, and all the wealth of the world is the result of brains.* A lump of gold would not have any value were it not for the brains which first enabled it to be wrought into something— coin or jewel, etc. The most precious substance in the universe today—radium—would not have been a penny a ton a century ago because brains had not discovered any use for it, and the same thing applies to everything. Evolve yourself and you make yourself of use; there is a need for you; you fill a position which only you can fill. It may take you some time, but what you gain is yours for all time. The enrichment of character means that new layers of yourself have been reached, and everything brought into manifestation must express itself, or, in other words, must act so that the added growth will open up opportunities you cannot foresee at present, and poverty will no longer affright.

As *like attracts like* so the poverty mind attracts poverty; and so long as the mind remains of that type so long must poverty be expressed in the environment. A locomotive made to run along on steel rails does the thing for which it was made; it cannot fly in the air or travel on water; a clock fulfils its functions by indicating time, but no one would expect it to record changes in the atmosphere. So with *mental states*. It is no use having ideals if the mind has not reached those levels where the ideals can be used. The mind that would have comfortable circumstances must always keep at a higher level, because by so doing the within thus created would find the without inadequate, *or not corresponding*, so the without would follow the within. Or a simpler illustration would be the pouring of a jelly into a mould. If the mould were misshapen or plain, so would be the shape of the jelly; if the mould were artistic or beautiful the jelly would have to pattern itself likewise.

When you grow a mind in which sufficiency, or plenty, *is the dominant thought,* in which the notion of poverty would appear so *grotesque,* so foreign to your nature as to be unthinkable, then you have created a mould, and the substance which will fill it—your circumstances or environment—*must follow the pattern. Truth gives rise to truth; a lie breeds lies; a rose produces a rose, not a thistle; good thoughts cannot produce bad actions;* everything fulfils the law of its being; an effect must be like its cause. *Sow thoughts of prosperity, by having faith in yourself, and you cannot reap anything but prosperity, but the thoughts must ever be of this type; to think now of poverty and then of prosperity will only yield indifferent results, for one neutralizes the other, as I have shown more than once in this book.* Reflect well over this truth: Poverty will not pass away until you create something better to take its place, and every man *can* create this *"something better."* Take courage; go in and win.

Twelve Affirmations for the Elimination of Poverty.

The following sentences will, if repeated with *understanding,* daily, bring about the change in consciousness which will eradicate completely doubt and the poverty habit.

The weakest man living has the powers of concentration folded *within his organization;* and they will remain folded *until he learns* to *believe* in their existence, and then tries to develop them.

To prepare for the life of opulence absolutely full of the power that draws wealth, *I must stand by the person I am.*

I *must* uphold my aim, by *believing* in myself, and never slacken one link of the good opinion I have formed of it.

Also know: each outreach of thy soul bears deep the seal of *cosmic impulse aeons.* That thing heart-hungry, every fibre thrills to reach, hath sought thee down the ages hungering, too.

You will never reach the place where you have all you want to spend except by *commanding yourself* to spend, and to want to spend, *less* than your income, whatever that may happen to be; for having all you want to spend is *a state of mind,* not a matter of hundreds, thousands or millions of dollars income.

It is literally true that you are what you think, and *when* you think, therefore think abundance always.

Every man gets just as much gold out of the world as he *puts into it.* All things are thought-made. Every man must *think his own gold into being.*

To him who believes he can, *everything* is an opportunity.

Depend only upon yourself, *believe* in yourself, but work in harmony with all things. Thus you call forth the *best* that is in yourself and secure the *best* that external sources have to give.

"The destruction of the poor is their poverty." The soul instinctively and rightly repels the idea of skimpiness.

Like the whirlwind and the waterspout I *twist* my environment into my form, whether it will or not.

Success from the most material to the most transcendental idea combines its power into a triad: *desire—expectation— preparation.*

"As a man believes, so is he." Even desultory thinking is *creative* and brings results. Premeditated and orderly thinking for a purpose *matures that purpose* into fixed form, so that you may be *absolutely sure* of the result of your dynamic experiment.

The Master Key

CHAPTER XXXVII.

LESSON THIRTY-FIVE.

THE ART OF GETTING RICH.

OPPORTUNITY IN A NEW LIGHT.

REAPING AND SOWING.

More and more is it being recognized that there is scarcely a single phase of existence which is not the result of the *immutable laws*. At one time it was believed that only the physical kingdom was under its sway; later it was seen that in the moral world *cause and effect*—heredity as it was termed —was paramount. Because the working of the law cannot be readily observed it does not follow that it is non-existent. The law of gravitation has always existed, although it was thousands of years before it was discovered, so in the same way there are many laws in the universe today of which we never dream. Psychology in the West is too modern a science to permit one to dogmatize as to its limitations, but in every realm of inquiry experience is teaching man that what he once regarded as *chaotic* is in reality an *ordered sequence;* that chance and luck are merely names invented to cover our ignorance of the underlying factors at work. Every thinking man and woman is forced to the conviction that justice rules the world; any other conception is impossible, yet were luck or chance (*the absence of which does not necessarily imply the presence of fate*) an actual force in the universe, justice would be incompatible with it. *Think this well over before proceeding any further, because its acceptance admits such immense possibilities.* A belief in it opens up a new world, and the *"unlucky,"* the downtrodden life's *"failures,"* the friendless, the outcast— all see in it undreamt of possibilities. Getting rich is as much under the domination of an immutable law as are the tides,

369

and in this most wonderful of all the centuries it will become manifest by the demonstrations of those who employ it. All successful men and women *obey this law,* though they do so *unconsciously,* for it is impossible to work outside it.

*No success is the result of chance,** though people will point to a single incident which served to raise an individual from poverty to affluence.

A man can only reap what he sows, and the stumbling across the opportunity has been prepared by the man himself previously, though he is probably unaware of it. The true inwardness of life can only be apprehended by the man who cognizes its operations upon *all* planes, and here and there such men have sprung up, shedding light upon what have hitherto been regarded as insoluble problems. As time goes on this class will increase, and more and more will the universality of law throughout Nature be proved. Within the last decade or two the science of metaphysics has been brought down to a practical working code for the everyday life of the man in the street, and every teacher of *Practical Psychology and Scientific Concentration* could show from his own experience or that of his fellow-students the truth of this. It is the application of this science with which many are concerned, and the application to the problems of daily life of a law which is unerring, and which places prosperity within the reach of every man or woman.

In Nature there is a constant tending of things from better to best, a proceeding from simplicity to complexity, but a complexity which means wider scope, more adaptability. We name this tendency Evolution, and it must not be restricted to the narrow sense in which it is generally used. Nature ever aims at perfection, an evolving, or expounding, so that more life may be expressed, and however slow this process may seem to the impatient reformer, who expects with a single act of congress to abolish poverty, crime, and injustice instantly, it is nevertheless very sure. Man can, however, delay the march forward; he can fall out of the ranks for the time being and rejoin later, but he *must* sometime or other obey the law of his being. A man of iron constitution may treat his body with impunity long past the period a more delicate man could, *but later he has to pay the penalty.*

**See, Faith In Self—Belief In Chance, Page 402.*

The purpose of evolution has not been recognized fully yet, so man has blundered along and created for himself *poverty and vice, disease and old age,* and thereby learned a much needed lesson—for all experience is but a lesson. He is beginning to wriggle out of it, and when he really desires a change he will get it.

Co-operation with nature is the point to aim at, for by so doing he achieves his true goal. There is one fact from which there is no getting away: *progress is eternal,* and man can help in this progress if he wishes.

There does not seem one epoch in the history of the world when the inhabitants of it were more *"alive"* than today. *Mental activity and industrial activity were surely never more intense!* Scarcely a plot of the earth's surface remains unmapped, and few regions that are at all hospitable but have been *"annexed"* by some government or other. We have vast continents in an undeveloped condition, and the wealth of the world continues to increase at a rapid rate. If there are more for the trade of the world there are more opportunities than ever there were. Life is far more complex; the wants of today have been a thousandfold increased as compared with those of our forefathers. As lesser evolved nations follow in the wake of *The United States and Europe*—and that they will is a foregone conclusion, *look at Japan*—more and more wealth will be created.

It is outside my purpose to consider whether all this leads to more happiness among humanity; the point is that where a century ago there was *one opportunity* today there are a *hundred* consequent upon our more complex civilization. This complexity is the outcome of the forces of evolution at work, and rightly interpreted, like pain and disease, are important factors in the advancement of man's conquest over his environment. Opportunity* is not that which comes once or twice in a man's lifetime, but something which may be created at pleasure. This superstititon has perhaps played more havoc with the human race in all ages in regard to getting on in life than that of any other. Quite a host of proverbs foster this delusion, such as, *"Every dog has his day."* *"There is a time in the affairs of men, which taken at the flood, leads on to*

---

*See Opportunity, (The First Opinion), and Opportunity, (The Second Opinion), Page 388.

fortune." Few men can say that they have not missed opportunities; we all do frequently, and it is galling when so many men become despondent and lose heart when they realize that they have allowed a splendid chance to slip through their fingers, especially if, as sometimes happens, it is apparently through no fault of their own.

The superstitions in which they have been cradled, *which obsessed their parents and great-grandparents, which confront them nearly every day of* their *lives among their fellows, thundered at them from the pulpits, emphasized in the literature of all nations and times, objectivised in the columns of the newspaper, in the records of crime and suicides, but above all, in one's own daily life—it is perhaps not surprising that the bogey of opportunity should bear the semblance of reality.* How many men have not fallen under the glamor of this gigantic illusion; when tired out with writing dozens of letters or tramping many weary miles and meeting with repeated failure to secure a berth, they have exclaimed, "It's just my luck"! You see, *the idea is so ingrained in one's make-up,* part of one's nature, that it seems very real. If I could convince you of its emptiness these pages would not have been written in vain, yet I do not hesitate to assert that opportunity is not a thing which fate provides for man, but *something created by man himself.* The limits of space do not permit the proof of this assertion being shown step by step, but that man is *master of his fate* has been proved by hundreds if not thousands of students of *"Concentration"* and *"Faith in Self" in America,* the home of the movement which is spreading over East and West rapidly, and destined in the not far distant future to revolutionize all our preconceived ideas of the world, man's place in it and his destiny. *This emancipation from the ogre of circumstances is not instantaneous;* it is a matter of growth, because it is based on law, outside which neither gods nor men are able to step.

We live in a veritable age of advancement, surmounted as we are by the triumphs of science and industry, but we are merely in the kindergarten of the powers of which men are now learning something. *Create your opportunities, but how?* By having belief in yourself. Remember that, "*to him that hath, faith in himself shall, be given; but him who hath no faith in himself, even that which he hath shall be taken away.*"

This truth, *"have faith in yourself,"* has been lost sight of except by a few, and they have not sought to force it upon a humanity which was not ready to receive it. Even today, with some, it is a matter of experiment, more or less. The ideas set forth here may not be fully appreciated by many, and for them the time has not arrived for the practical using of their thought-force. Even otherwise intelligent literary critics have shown a deplorable want of knowledge on the most elementary laws of practical metaphysics; luckily for their bumptiousness their opinions are in cold type, so that the world will be able later to measure their ignorance by the demonstrated powers of thought. A sign of the times is the thousands of students of Concentration.

HE CAN WHO THINKS HE CAN.

He can who thinks he can. Here is the burden of this *Chapter,* and were it expanded to a thousand pages it could only reiterate the fact. Now let us see if there is any connection between what precedes this section. We have on the one hand a busy world, daily expanding, on the lookout for men with brains, willing to pay handsomely for them. Such princely salaries were unknown in by-gone days, because then there were not the possibilities there are today. There are plenty of third-rate men—the market is glutted with them, but on all hands it is admitted that men *can not be found* to fill the responsible positions which are waiting to be filled.

Why is it the age of young men? Why are young fellows ousting men of experience in large and important business houses? Because the spirit of progress is in the air. New times *demand* new methods, and when men attain a certain age their minds like their bodies ossify, become incapable of admitting the wave of new ideas which is spreading over the world. Old age affects temperament, and does not favor the permeation of ideas quickly, except here and there, where a mind well up in age is tuned to a certain pitch to catch the vibrations.

The root of the problem lies in one's mentality. Most men take themselves as they are. They believe that they are limited in certain directions and therefore they never attempt to transcend those limitations. It stands to common sense that if a man has not a good opinion of himself no one else will have. The world takes a man at his own valuation, and if he labels himself a nobody the world is scarcely to be blamed for believing it. A man is *fettered* in circumstances because he is fettered in mind first.

The mental outlook determines the physical one.

One's circumstances are always the visible result of one's thought. All actions are the outcome of our thoughts, therefore our environment is self-created.

Some men like to *think* they are the victims of circumstances, as it saves them a lot of trouble; they can then *remain* quiescent, and put forth no new effort. When things go wrong, *as they inevitably must* under such circumstances, they turn round and say: "It's just what I expected—everything's against me."

Man has usually been hypnotized by the belief that he is the result of his environment—the sport of fate—what wonder when this is the attitude adopted that he *cripples the aspirations* which would lead him to better and higher things. Such a view of life *must* affect his progress, because *a man is that which he believes he is.* While this distorted view is held he fetters himself, because he is then incapable of formulating ideas which would give him financial freedom. Everything which enters the avenues of the senses produces impressions, and it is within man's power to *refuse* admission to any set of impressions. An undesirable element may crop up in his environment, but he may forbid its entering his mind, and so long as he prevents undesirable thoughts or things—*both are much the same*—from entering his consciousness he cannot be affected by adverse conditions. The mind cannot follow two trains of thought at the same time, and at the centre of the mind man is perfectly free to initiate or originate any thought he likes. It is only on the *periphery,* as it were, that he is at the mercy and impressions and thoughts of others, and so long as he centres his usual consciousness on this outside so long must he expect to be lacking in originality, force, judgment, and resourcefulness, without which prosperity cannot successfully be wooed. The *periphery* of the mind is made up of the scum of the current thought of the day of Tom, Dick and Harry, of the common garden man, who thanks his stars he is like the rest of his fellows. The owner is pleased to call it *his* mind; it is the unconscious receptacle of any thoughts of a similar nature.

Man alone possesses the power to *either accept or reject thoughts,* and it is by virtue of this fact that we have such a multiplicity of objects around us. It is the presence of the marvellous inventions and the extraordinary advances made by modern science that demonstrates this unique power. Only one greater power can be possessed by any creature—*the ability to create thought.* The man who can initiate thought is the man who has the world at his feet. Analyze the conversation round you daily and you will never by any chance hear an original thought, because everyone thinks from the outside of his mind, not the centre. Yet that centre exists, and it is the receptacle of the most precious gem the world can imagine. Its presence is unexpected because it has never been developed.

It has been taken for granted that a man was what Nature made him, that the brain he was born with could not be enlarged in its powers. Yet every day this view is demonstrated to be false. *Dull boys have become brilliant men; lads, the sons of laborers,* showing no marked ability even when manhood was reached, *have startled the world* by their achievements in science, art, commerce or literature. Their fellow men have regarded them as being geniuses, as being born with the faculties which have made them famous.

Many a poor farmer boy has given the true source of the powers displayed, and genius is *only a capacity* for taking pains; so in the same way every man may be clever in some direction or other if he only desires to be. Some men who have been absorbed in some pursuit have found that it did not yield the success they sought. It is possible in such cases to so develop their thought that ways and means will suggest themselves for improving to the fullest the gifts they have created by their own efforts.

"He hasn't got it in him," is a common expression applied to some men, *yet these same men when driven to extremities have risen above circumstances.*

The policy of ninety-nine men out of a hundred is to drift. When they have learned their calling they take no more interest in it, and at that point stagnation begins. *A man cannot stand still. The order of Nature is eternal progress,* and as man is the highest product of Nature he is a participator in this onward march. He can delay his evolution if he wishes, as already stated, but he cannot prevent it. On the other hand, he can hasten it immensely by understanding the laws. One expression of this eternal progress is the demand for the best. Even poor people want the best, whatever it be. One of the causes assigned for the falling off of *Canadian* trade with *England* is that the goods are not packed as tidily and nicely as those of *American* and other competitors. There is a sense of beauty arising in even humble quarters among people one would suppose to be quite indifferent. The public is more exacting in its demands, and what was good enough for our forefathers is not good enough for us. Criticism was never more rife among every section of the community than today; no one and nothing can escape it, and the quickened intelligence is spreading among all classes. The tendency of the age is a desire for more freedom, a wider life, a broader outlook. *There is desire for more power. Discontent is evident on all hands.* There is a dissatisfaction with things as they exist at present, and the world is filled with organizations to remedy evils of every kind.

Enough has been said to show the existence of a factor which is pushing man on, and it is a law that the *presence of a desire is evidence of the provision of means to express that desire.* The desire to be prosperous is a *perfectly legitimate one;* those who in the old days *"took the vow of poverty"* no doubt accomplished the development they sought along other lines, but poverty under present-day conditions is a very different thing, and there is nothing to recommend it. The glamor and romance which once surrounded it have disappeared.

In a world which is, as has been said, daily increasing in wealth and must continue to increase, until every square yard of the earth that can be tilled or exploited has rendered its service to man, there is no necessity for poverty. No one need be poor, nor need anyone be governed by circumstances. Every man may make his own.

The primary step to be taken is the creation of a desire or wish to reach some point; without this riches will not trouble anyone. While there is, as stated above, considerable discontent in the world with present conditions there is a large class of persons who regard contentment as the one virtue to be cultivated above all others. They try to believe that happiness and contentment are synonymous, because somebody somewhere and at some time said or taught so. That is sufficient. They tell each other of this, and by dint of assiduously endeavoring to believe it contentment is sanctified.

In this way some of the greatest humbugs and illusions of the ages have acquired an odor of truth and respectability. Contentment is one of them. When a man is quite content he is on the down grade. He has ceased to grow. So long as growth remains in animal or plant stagnation is impossible. The meaning of growth is desire to express the individual or nature, and once that end has been attained there is a gradual decadence, simply because there is nothing more to express. Nature will not tolerate lumber, and the man who believes he has exhausted his powers is removed from the scene of his operations. *He signs his own death warrant.* It has frequently been remarked how business men who have retired and had no hobby have not long survived their new existence.

The creation of a desire is not difficult, but there must be clearness in the desire and persistency in holding it, because if the desire is *nebulous* and *spasmodic* the man will not work understandingly, and the prosperity will be very haphazard. He must outlive the good he has in view, and if this is adhered to it will materialize.

As mind exists for the expression of the man, so once a man has created by his thought an environment, that environment must surround him sooner or later. No power on earth can keep it away from him. He may delay its consummation, because he will have to outwear the causes he has set going, but every cause must be exhausted some time. As soon as a man has realized in his consciousness the goal he aims at people and things instrumental to his success *will be magnetically drawn to him,* for like attracts like on every plane. Many instances of this could be cited were space sufficient. By the creation of new desires new thoughts and ideas will spring into being, and by nursing these ideas *"ways and means"* will occur, and the man will say, "I wonder I never thought of this before." When *Edison* wishes to get light on a problem he just sits still and thinks quietly until the knowledge comes. Intuition is a real force in every human being, but thanks to the "practical" attitude taken everywhere it has been almost stifled. The genius and the inventor get flashes now and then which illuminate them for the moment, and any man or woman could do the same if he or she cultivated the power. Concentration, as students have told me, has made them over again, and the individual of little intelligence need not despair, for the whole of the consciousness cannot manifest at once.

Consciousness is like an iceberg—the portion which is seen, corresponding to the ordinary consciousness, is only a tithe of the real size of the berg, which is hidden away in the depths of the water.

Many a man who has passed forty or fifty, who has not led an active mental life, gets it into his head that he is too old to pull his brains together, that it is all very well for a young fellow. Suppose, for instance, he decides to improve his education, and commences to take up the study of some subject. He is brought into touch with new terms, strange words, and lines of thought quite foreign to him. He finds his mind muddled, to use his own words, and he gives the study up, disgusted. He either comes to the conclusion that he is not cut out for study, or that he is too old to begin to learn.

Both suppositions are wrong. Any teacher will tell him that it is the universal experience that when new subjects are taken up the mind rebels because it is against that law which proclaims that the path of non-resistance is always the easiest. Water will always select a channel before ground strewn with obstacles, and a man who has always done a habitual act with the right hand will experience great difficulty and awkwardness if he uses the left. *Every thought marks a channel in the brain, or effects a certain area, and when a new channel is to be dug there are many difficulties to surmount.*

A little patience and persistence will enable any man to take himself in hand, and he may take up the study of anything he chooses.

Going back to what has been said, he will see that his mind is undisciplined, that it has *"bossed"* him up to now, and that naturally it resents being taken in hand, and compelled to go along a certain line.

Once desire has been awakened the mind will cast about for some means to achieve the end it has in view, and provided it is not damped by race-thought it will mature plans which will inevitably bring to pass the goal sought. When it is remembered that every one of the millions of cells of which our body is composed has a consciousness all its own, quite independent of that of the body—often termed by some schools of psychologists the *"group consciousness,"* and that each atom before it disintegrates, has the power of handing over as a legacy to the incoming tenant its own rate of vibration, it will be understood why all of us possess different natures. It will also explain why the things we would do we are unable to accomplish—at first. Thanks to the law of change, which permeates every part of Nature, there is no characteristic possessed by any human being which cannot be absolutely transformed, which accounts for the startling changes seen in some people. Even the *"eternal hills"* are never a moment at rest. Particle by particle changes, molecule by molecule, *undergoes transformation,* and in the interior of the earth the same changes are taking place. Life and motion are the same thing, so-called rest being but a change of motion. It is useful to remember these facts of exact science, because they are so pertinent to the matter we are dealing with at present.

As every force acts along the line of least assistance, the forces of mind inevitably flow along those channels which have been *carved by habit,* and habit is but another name for race-thought, plus environment and education. When one applies common sense to *Concentration*—and this is its very basis—the miraculous elements with which it is credited assume their proper proportions, and any thoughtful man is bound to accept the main propositions of the *new Psychology.* New channels can always be made, and as the old ones are not used they dry up, as it were, or become obliterated in time, and thoughts flow just as easily along the used ones. Keeping this in view and the fact that the surface of the brain has always areas which are like blank phonographic records, the student will understand the need of application.

The direction of a desire will be unconsciously guided along some line for which there is some taste. There is not a human being who has not some taste or tendency. If these appear to be general, and you cannot make up your mind which you should cultivate to the exclusion of the others, do not worry about the thing, but sit alone at intervals and have a good think with yourself. Try and cultivate a receptive attitude, and often you will find an idea will flash into your mind that will appeal to you instinctively as being worth noting. By dismissing it, or allowing the thought to be turned out by an obtruding thought is to render its reappearance less probable, so that you should *determine that* you are going to *"think it up"* for all it is worth.

Practical reverie of this kind is a necessary factor in prosperity building, for many suggestions undreamt of will occur spontaneously. Your brain, attuned to certain vibrations, will intercept similar vibrations, of other minds by a well-known law of psychology, just as telegraphic or wireless messages are intercepted at times.

Having nursed your desires and found your own line, you will find that after all questions as to ways and means are not so difficult. When this stage is reached a course of reading of biographies of successful men should be undertaken. The material for this class of literature is easily accessible nowadays, and some "points" will soon be picked up. The presence in nearly every case *of belief in oneself* will suggest to the reader that this is an essential—almost the first essential.

Some writers make belief the starting point, but I have always doubted the wisdom of this plan, as belief is one of the hardest things to induce, without a motive, and desire supplies this. *Want of belief* has stood in the way of achievement in so many times, even in the case of earnest students that anything which will make it more easily obtained is worth considering. Going carefully over what has been said, one will become increasingly familiar with the line of thought, and it will gradually work itself into the consciousness until it becomes part of his very being. What has so long been wanting has been a reason for things, and existing systems of thought training have not provided this. The point which the universe has reached in evolution at present enables any thoughtful observer to apprehend the why and the wherefore in a manner which would be utterly incomprehensible to our forefathers, who could only deduce from what they saw around them. The wider and grander interpretation of the *cosmos* was only possible to men of the twentieth century, because the unfolding in the past had not proceeded at so rapid a rate as in this "wonderful century," when things are accelerated in every direction.

Belief being a matter which is within everyone's power to increase as he will, provided he only goes about it the right way, the student need not lose heart, because he does not achieve results rapidly. Remember that it is the same with thought as it is with food: it is not the quantity supplied to the organism, but the quantity which is assimilated that counts. *Confidence is begot in oneself by carrying out whatever policy one decides upon; in other words, belief is of a twofold nature —thought and action.* It is only by doing things that one comes to actually believe, and ability to achieve increases with every action performed. Begin to think better of yourself, for it is generally the people who have a poor opinion of themselves that never get anywhere. Their belief works itself out in their character, their demeanor, showing itself even in physical characteristics, such as the walk, position of the head, the carriage, the expression. Cast to the winds those enslaving old saws which used to console the failures of the past, and rob them of initiative. Knowing something of the times in which they were coined, they were the natural outcome of the age, the expression of the mental life. Authority is responsible for the *self-condemnation* and disbelief in one's self which has spread over so many people.

Make a new start. Learn to trust in yourself. You may make mistakes at first; but the more you cultivate your intuitions and rely upon them the greater will become your reliance in your own power. When a voice speaking in *England* or *France* can be heard in *America* without any visible means of connection it is not taxing your credulity to ask you to believe that space is filled by thought vibrations of various types, and that one is automatically switched on to the type which is thinking along the same lines. The success of all experiments in wireless telegraphy or telephony depends upon harmony between transmitter and receiver. Both being tuned to the same key the waves of ether carry the vibrations set up by the transmitter to the receiver, which is keyed to respond to those particular vibrations.

Now I will split up, for purposes of illustration, the *thought-atmosphere* into layers of differing density. The heavy, sluggish layers may be regarded as representing the thought found in the majority of the people. This layer will be composed of ordinary dull-as-ditchwater thought, and when a man is content with an uncongenial environment his thoughts sink down to this level. When he is inclined to be retrospective this murky sea of thought surges round his brain. He unconsciously absorbs and stores away in his mental storehouse masses of this destructive thought. The more he stored away the more frequent would be the habit of chewing the cud of bitter reflections, and his brain-machine would respond more readily to the vibrations of this lowest level of thought. This would produce a state of mind where he felt that he must let loose the accumulated mass of thought, to gain relief, and he would *"yearn for sympathy."* To whom would he unbosom his troubles? Should he go to the successful man, the prosperous merchant? No, because he would be unappreciative; he would fail to *"understand"* him. The optimist would cheer him up, and he would feel that it was not exactly what he wanted at that moment. A callous man could not give him the aid he sought, so he would seek solace from some one who had experienced the same difficulties he had passed through. How common are such instances?

"Birds of a feather"—*"Like attracts like."*

He who would be prosperous *must avoid* the unlucky, the unfortunate, for the sympathy they receive in this direction but *fetters* them more closely, as it keeps their mentality on the low plane it should have risen above.

Raise the thoughts by determination not to succumb to the temptation of dwelling upon actual conditions. These were the result of previous thought, *and so the future is being woven of the fabrics of the present*—your thought, for, as the student must again be reminded, all action is preceded by thought. By the initial impulse you *raise your mentality* to another higher plane, and every time you succeed in doing this you strengthen your thought by the accession of analogous thoughts, thoughts from the minds of men who have scaled the heights of prosperity. You catch or intercept their thought currents, strengthening and solidifying your own mental structure. Unused brain areas will now be brought under contribution. Having created new permanent channels it will not be found difficult to maintain them, *and belief in yourself* will have been achieved—the one great task which renders the accomplishment of all else comparatively simple.

I will now consider some additional factors in the *Law of Prosperity,* and in the forefront of these must be placed *Concentration.* Every time the mind wanders off bring it back. Avoid abstract ideas when exercising for the acquirement of this faculty. Concrete examples should be taken, which the everyday life offers. It is infinitely easier to *concentrate* on that in which we are interested.

Let that subject be your work, whatever it may be. Let your work be representative of yourself, and your best self at that. If you are an employee concentrating on your work it will be more thoroughly done and you are unwittingly fitting yourself for a higher position. It will insensibly lead to your taking a live interest in your work, and if this is done it will make you a better workman. Doing a thing because it is your livelihood, and doing it because you love to do it, are two widely different things, and he who loves his work never finds time hang heavily upon his hands. He rarely gets tired, and hence extracts a joy from his daily duties which the artificial pleasures of theatre or ball do not yield to their devotees. It follows that equability and calmness will be built into the nature, and, incidentally, the health will be improved; good health will be needed, unless one be left a fortune, and even then riches without it will not benefit one much. Besides, the doing of a thing well fits a man to undertake more responsible work, and if his present employment does not offer this he will find the opportunity later, or create it himself.

A good memory is a necessity, and concentration is an important aid. Mind-wandering, or the dissipation of mental energy, which is so commonly found in the unsuccessful in life, is more effectively corrected by concentration than by anything else, and one secret of concentration is interest—a real, living, intense, whole-hearted interest. This is a quality which is generally very colorless in the man who lacks riches. If he has any live interest it is not of a constructive type, but takes his mind along channels which do not accomplish anything. As a rule a man who is wholly absorbed in a subject has a good memory as regards that particular topic.

He retains a mass of facts and figures which applied to another subject would make him an expert. So he who would acquire the *Art of Getting Rich* must cultivate his memory. A promise once made must be fulfilled, for the old-time excuse of a bad memory may pass occasionally, but it will not always be accepted. More money is lost through a bad memory than is supposed. Many a good order which would have led to larger ones has been lost through failure to call upon a customer or send him some data required. We in the West are always too ready to promise because we do not wish to displease our friends, but one should be very chary in giving one's word, when there is not much probability of carrying out what you have pledged to do.

Do not imagine that it is a good plan to improve a bad memory by relying upon it for a mass of details which it has no right to contain. Modern life gives us myriads of facts and things to remember with which our forefathers never had to trouble themselves, with the result that there is a far greater tax upon the power of recollecting. There is no particular virtue in loading up the memory with trivialities, things which the mind cannot use for any purpose, therefore these small things should be delegated to a notebook. Have no fear that the mind will be weakened thereby. Rather will it leave it the freer to attend to the really important things, for, after all, the really important things one does in a day's work are few; the bulk of the time of many is spent in "pottering about." Even the day's work of many a so-called busy man could be boiled down to a couple of hours, through a want of system and method, and a paying of time and attention to insignificant things quite out of proportion to the necessities of the case. With the use of a notebook commences order, system, the delegation of duties to their proper quarter, the saving of time which can well be devoted to the working out of problems which bear on the fact of your advancing, and the conservation of mental energy which would otherwise be exhausted. A prominent cause of failure in modern life is the worry habit, and this is induced as much by a multiplicity of details as by anything else. The man who would solve the problem of riches must be of a calm temperament, but the man who worries has a mind alien to this requirement.

With the relief of the mind from little matters the memory can readily be trained to respond, and to yield up whatever is required of it. Then the full meaning of that oft-quoted phrase: *"His word is as good as his bond,"* will carry weight with it. No man can rely upon himself alone altogether. Put a man in the *Sahara* desert and he might remain there all his life and never be a cent more in pocket. Put him, on the other hand, where there are a number of men, and it is certain that some one will want his help or counsel in some way. Man is naturally a gregarious animal, and he is a dissatisfied one, too. That is, he is always wanting something which he thinks will minister to his comfort. It is this very never-content attitude which evolves him, and as he may plan or theorize to secure more of these comforts he has to invoke the aid of his fellowmen in some shape. Man, being a bundle of wants, is the safeguard of his getting on. Through it new industries spring into existence every day, new luxuries or necessities, according to the view taken, arise, and the demand must be met. The man in request will be he who anticipates the wants or demands of his fellows. History teems with examples of men of this type, and the evocation of faculties which perfect the judgment will show what is wanted and how best to supply it. It is the man with ideas that the world wants, and whatever he asks will be given him.

It is a common thing to hear an unsuccessful man say: "If I only had scope I would not be where I am now." As a matter of fact the position he was in furnished all scope necessary, *but he had failed to recognize or utilize it.*

When a man fails to win out in a position he has been in for years, the cause is not in the position, but the man.

Experience confirms this every day. Two men will carry on the same kind of business in the same street, and, to all appearances, conditions will be equal for both. After some years one will have built up a good business and the other will be where he was, marking time, as it were, or have lost ground. The fault is not business being overcrowded, for one business is as good as another.

When *Baron Rothschild* was importuned by an anxious mother as to which business gave the best results, he replied, *"Selling matches is as good as any other, provided you sell plenty."*

It is method which tells, the way of looking at things, the mental attitude, in short. If a man can really believe he can make a business a success he will do so, but he has to be steeped to the ears in this belief. Once he gets on fire with the notion, the obstacles which meet him become very minor matters. The feeling that he can make the thing *"go"* brings forth all that is in him.

Unsuspected suggestions will occur to him; for one thing he will clear out of the time-honored ruts which his forefathers always followed so assiduously. He knows that there must ever be wants of some kind, and there is no logical reason why he can not supply those wants. He is not, of course, bound to stay in a business or a position he does not like, but the fact that he finds himself where he is shows that he is not fit for a bigger position. Once he is ready for a more responsible position he will gravitate towards it, provided he has the desire to; but the fault with the majority of people is that once having reached some point which they have always regarded as their objective, they have not placed a further goal in its place, so no further headway is made.

The business chosen, then, is almost immaterial: the cardinal point is the manner in which it is carried on. Many of the most successful businesses of the world have been created in the first instance by a winning personality, and where there is not much capital to commence with this is an invaluable asset. The laws of attraction and repulsion, which are seen even as low in the scale of Evolution as minerals, reaches its culmination in man. The man who repels his fellowmen is not the man who is likely to make a big success at anything. Even a genius or clever inventor cannot dispense entirely with his fellows. Help or co-operation of some sort is necessary, and it is only when a vast organization has been built up that the personal influences may be discounted. Exclusiveness, aloofness, reserve have been the stumbling-block of many really clever men who could have marketed their ability had they gone about it the right way.

It is not always that there is no scope, but that a man may be in a calling he has no taste for. In such a case he can make the best he can of the circumstances, and when opportunity occurs leave it. No man can be a big success in any vocation which he dislikes. Everything in connection with it is done perfunctorily. He cannot put his heart and mind into it, therefore his *best* is lacking, and only when the best is put into a thing does it yield its highest results.

If all men followed the *nomadic* life that is still practiced by some tribes in the *East* there would be small room for initiative. The wants of the tribe would be few; food, shelter and clothing would be sufficient. Thanks to modern civilization a thousand avenues are open to the man of today—art, science, commerce, in their innumerable combinations. Every day new industries spring up, new minerals or materials are discovered, new uses for old things spring to light, and the future will be still more remarkable in this respect. All this means countless opportunities, and the glib talk of there being no equality of opportunity is sheer nonsense. The man at the bottom is not there because he has not had any opportunities, but because he is not fit to be anywhere else.

It is futile to talk of abolishing slums by legislation so long as slum minds exist.

Poverty is no hindrance to riches, often it is the greatest aid. If you doubt this statement look at the lives of the rich men of the world—the *multi-millionaires*. How many of them began life with wealth, education, influential friends?

The world is changing its thought; in the past, those who believed in *The Art of Getting Rich,* were among the isolated few, and were looked upon with suspicion by the many; in the present, the great majority desire to take advantage of *"Opportunity"* and most of these believe it is possible.

This change of thought is due to the fact, that earnest men and women, are fast *eliminating* the term *"impossible"* from their vocabulary.

Many are now convinced that life is not made for poverty and disease; they now believe that these are but a temporary creation of man gone astray.

They do not believe that this world is a *"vale of tears,"* nor that we must suffer in the present in order that we may gain bliss in the future. We do not gather figs from thistles, neither can a life of poverty and disease be the direct cause of a life of pleasure. It is an immutable law that like causes produce like effects, and many are beginning to intelligently use this law in shaping their life and destiny.

The source of all riches is within. There is no more difficulty in becoming rich than there is in becoming clever in a business or profession, only some men find the secret more easily than others.

Adverse circumstances never yet held down a man who was determined to rise. The more insuperable the difficulties the more powerful has the man become who has emerged from them.

All the enemies a man has to contend with are of his own creation. One by one he can vanquish them if he will.

What man has done man can do.

What is the one desideratum in the acquirement of wealth? Talent? Not exactly. Some very talented men have been very poor. Education? No, there are *plenty* of educated men miserably poor.

Trust in ourselves must come first. After that all is secondary. This is the common asset of every wealthy man. Luck, fate, chance, opportunity have no claim to consideration. All men and women, with very few exceptions, *are hypnotized by them. Opportunity,* surely, you may say, plays some part?

Contrast the two following *opinions* respecting *"opportunity"* on the next page. The opinion expressed in the *first* you are probably familiar with, but the opinion expressed in the *second* is not so well known:

OPPORTUNITY.

THE FIRST OPINION.

Master of human destinies am I,
Fame, love, and fortune on my footsteps wait.
Cities and fields I walk: I penetrate
Deserts and seas remote, and passing by
Hovel, and mart, and palace—soon or late
I knock unbidden once at every gate.
If sleeping, wake—if feasting, rise before
I turn away. It is the hour of fate,
And they who follow me reach every state
Mortals desire, and conquer every foe
Save death: but those who doubt or hesitate,
Condemned to failure, penury, and woe;
Seek me in vain and uselessly implore—
I answer not, and I return no more.

OPPORTUNITY.

THE SECOND OPINION.

They do me wrong who say I come no more
  When once I knock and fail to find you in;
For every day I stand outside your door,
  And bid you wake, and rise to fight and win.
Wail not for precious chances passed away,
  Weep not for golden ages on the wane;
Each night I burn the records of the day,
  At sunrise every soul is born again.
Dost thou behold thy lost youth all aghast?
  Dost reel from righteous retribution's blow?
Then turn from blotted achives of the past,
  And find the future's pages *white as snow.*
Art thou a mourner? *Rouse thee from thy spell;*
  Art thou a sinner? *Sins may be forgiven;*
Each morning gives thee wings to flee from hell,
  Each night a star to guide thy feet to heaven!
Laugh like a boy at splendors that have sped,
  To vanished joys be blind and deaf and dumb;
My judgments seal *the dead past with its dead,*
  But never bind a moment yet to come.
Though deep in mire, wring not your hands and weep;
  I lend my arm to all who say: "I can."
No shamefaced outcast ever sank so deep
  But yet might rise and be again a man.

In the *first* opinion *opportunity* is shown as coming, or knocking but once at every mortal's door, and if you follow it you will reach every state mortals desire, save death; but if you hesitate you are condemned to failure, penury and woe. You seek *opportunity* in vain; it answers not, and returns no more if you fail to take advantage of it.

In the *second* opinion it is shown that *opportunity* stands outside and *knocks every day* at man's door, and bids him wake and rise up to fight and win. *Opportunity* is also shown as lending its arm to all who say, *"I can,"* and that you *can rise again and be a man.*

Needless to say that the writer *believes literally* in the opinion of *opportunity,* as set forth in the *second opinion,* and that those who have *faith and confidence* in themselves take advantage of opportunity whenever it comes.

Sincere, honest desire is the star that leads one to opportunities; while *"faith and belief"* in one's self enables the confident man or woman to take advantage of *"the opportunity,"* at any time.

Right here, faithful student, I again ask you to read all of this chapter over again, for the ideas being new will require some repetition before they can effectually bring you to take action. But you may object and say, I am only an average sort of a person, I am not gifted with any special ability. This is because you have not *"discovered"* yourself. You have got it into your head that having grown up you are what you were as a child, plus the result of experience and environment. But you are infinitely more than this, as I have already shown. *Your abilities are latent, like the strength that lies coiled up potentially in the muscles of everyone.*

It is action which brings forth the strength. So it is putting into practice the abilities that you will evoke from yourself that will enable you to reach the goal you have in view. Ability is undeniably required in building up a fortune, but this ability may be cultivated. You were perhaps put into some business because either your father was in it before you, or you thought you would like it. At twenty or thirty one does not always know what one likes; sometimes one does not discover one's life-work till forty and after that age—and then one thinks that as one is doing that kind of work it would be better perhaps to go on doing it for all time. How is it possible to find out what is in one, when that attitude is taken? *"The*

Great Within" has never been suspected except in the case of our great men, yet in this is a literal and figurative gold mine for every human being.   Millions pass through life never suspecting that as one of the wise books of the *East* says:

"Within thyself must deliverance be sought."

Hero-worship *Diminishes Heroes;* every man is *potentially a hero, or a great man,* in some direction or other, but it usually requires a crisis to make the fact patent.   No sane man dare place a limit on man's powers, for, as a matter of exact science, *no limit* has ever been found.

The oldest, and, at the same time, newest of sciences—psychology—has never had a fair trial.   Its consideration has always been a purely academic one, never dreaming that it had another side, and that it was one of the most practical and matter-of-fact sciences of which we had any conceptions.

By trusting in yourself you provide those conditions which will reveal and bring forth your ability.   No two human minds are the same, and if you regard yourself as commonplace your mind has taken you at your own estimate until all you think and do is commonplace, lacking resource, initiative, originality. The habit of trusting in yourself, of *believing* you are capable of much more will enable the mind within to give you new light on problems around you, and that indefinite thing—*ability,* will grow day by day.

It may sound strange to learn that *man has power to create any circumstances he desires,* but it is nevertheless a fact, and is being demonstrated constantly by students who have taken up practical metaphysics.   Generally the fault is that a man does not know what he really does desire.   This week or year it is this thing, next year it is something else, hence he rarely realizes his ideals.   The man who would be wealthy must let this thought dominate his whole being.   He must satisfy himself that he really does know what he desires.

Too many people entertain a vague feeling that they would like this, that, or the other: this attitude must be altered.

They must examine themselves carefully and find out what they actually do want first.   It would be foolish to say: *"I should like to be rich,"* without having something to be rich for.   If a *Hottentot* were given a cheque for one hundred thousand dollars it would not raise him in the slightest; if it were given to many a civilized man it would spell physical and moral ruin. No, a man who would be rich must have evolved sufficiently in order to have a use for those riches. If he has no leanings to culture, to travel, to surround himself with the beautiful, to express outwardly what marks his growth inwardly, or no wish to benefit those of his fellow-creatures who have not reached the same point he has, then the pursuit would be abortive and unmoral, for all men are brothers; all have a common origin, and whatever raises one without in some measure raising his fellows re-acts prejudicially. The unrest of the modern world is struggling to voice this fact.

The smarting sense of injustice to one section of the community through its inability to protect itself from the rapacity of another section becomes daily more articulate, more pronounced.

Examine your motives with the keenest scrutiny, and once convinced of their honesty take the plunge. Begin to develop yourself systematically. Cultivate an unconquerable ambition, an indomitable doggedness that you *will* accomplish the end in view. The desire must be one that is not to be swept away with the first obstacle that presents itself. The word *"impossible"* must be erased from the tablets of your mind. Your goal must stand out as clearly as the outlines of a city behind which the pale moon is rising, *silhouetted* against the heavens. Blurred ideals, ideals lost in a diffusive mistiness never materialize because of their want of cohesion, of definiteness, of persistency.

The Law of Wealth.

How will the riches come, you may ask? Never mind for the moment. You have made up your mind that you are going to climb the path to prosperity: leaving the working out to your interior forces. As has just been said there are innumerable walks in life which the one-sided, narrow existence of our forefathers rarely dreamt of. It may be through invention, through the employment of a gift which has long lain in the recesses of the mind unsuspected, through what *you* may call "accident" or "luck," but, remember: *whatever you create mentally is absolutely certain to express itself outwardly.* This is the Law; you doubt it? Look at any man who is not well-to-do. Is he accustomed when considering finance to think in six figures? Does he not as the head of the household, often say: *"We can't afford this; this is too dear?"* Is he not ever seeking to economize along this line or that, or complaining, if in business, of the heavy rates, and the increasing cost of things, and the keenness of competition which will eventually drive him out of the place?

I do not assert that every man who is not wealthy talks like this, but I do say that all who *think* poverty *express* poverty. Getting into close contact with the poor will show that they never hold large ideas concerning money, and usually consider themselves incapable of organizing and conducting large concerns. They depreciate themselves, and therefore never rise above the average in regard to money. You will rarely hear them speak of what they intend to do in the future. Seldom will they go beyond a "wish," which usually is expressed thus: *"I wish I could find a lot of money."* Most successful men become so with no knowledge of the Law—it is done unconsciously, therefore one does not often hear of their saying beforehand what they intend being or doing. *Andrew Carnegie* and one or two other self-made men have put this on record, but I do not remember coming across any other instances. What I am seeking is the case of practical dreamers, who are naturally few and far between. I could cite instances of students who have put the *Law* into operation and benefited accordingly, but the best example which will be known to most people is the conception found in fiction in the character of *Svengali*. You will remember that when he was in the direst straits and could not pay his rent he would say: "One day I shall be rich: I shall have a carriage, a big fur coat, and even princes will pay me homage." He held to this ideal in spite of the squalor which seemed as though it would always surround him. He had an *unquenchable faith* in himself, and dreamed daily of the future that he planned.

This is the system upon which one should proceed. Ignore present conditions utterly; live in an atmosphere of plenty, whatever be your actual environment. You create your future from the present, just as the present is the outcome of the past. Do not postpone, even in thought, the advent of riches. Act as though you were already wealthy, that you had achieved the goal in view, then the wish which takes foundation will have passed into *expectancy,* which is a very different attitude, something far beyond even hope.

From what has been said it follows that *one must practice constructive thinking,* which is a very different thing from ordinary thought, a haphazard, happy-go-luck way of thinking. By constructive thinking you have a purposive plan where before you had no plan whatever, where the thought was merely drift, whatever presented itself to the mind. A thought repeated has a tendency to recur more readily according as the mind may be at liberty, or not disciplined. Discipline is always suggestive of something unpleasant, of duty, of something which runs in the face of the line of least resistance. A strong body results from use, from exercise, and even a robust and physically perfect body would lose its virility, its strength, by not being used. 'The case of the mind is just the same. The forceful, purposive mind can only result from ordered and trained thinking. The conception of training thought is a novelty to most people, but it is just as rational as training the fingers to play the piano like a *Padcrewski;* the difference between the budding pianist, represented by the average man, and the artist, is a question of time. His skill is not a gift, the only gift he possessed was an *unshakeable determination* to master the task he had set himself, and an aptitude for hard work, and without these no man may hope to get rich.

There are too many people who are always seeking a quick-get-rich method, and are doomed to disappointment, for Nature never gives something for nothing. There is an increasing number who yearn for opulence, but who never raise a finger to obtain it, and it cannot be too plainly said that there is no magic, no mysteries in the lines laid down here, *merely a using of the materials every human being possesses.* The world is ever looking for the new, the latest, the great things, and it pays handsomely for them. Evolution being a progression, conditions are always undergoing modifications, and natural resources are more and more taxed. The mere fact of the invention of the *motor car* has led to the use of vast capital for the growing of rubber; the same cause has led another brain to attempt the solution of an adequate supply by the invention of a substitute for rubber, much cheaper. Such illustrations can be multiplied easily, and it is open to any man or woman to anticipate the wants of the world and provide them.

By constructive thought the faculties of the mind which have long lain dormant will be roused into activity, and in this rousing an expansion of the normal consciousness results. This gives an utterly new outlook upon life. As thought becomes constructive all the old poverty-stricken ideas will die out. Circumstances have always dictated the type of thinking. A man in financial difficulties, if he is of a sunny or careless type, may treat them lightly, or even *philosophically,* but from time to time his environment compels him to face the situation. This brings his mind in line with the orthodox thought, and in this way old thought is maintained. The habitual outlook upon life is kept intact; the self-made manacles are riveted the firmer about the victim who treads the old path, follows in the rut which the feet of countless millions have trodden. A standard is formed, and every thought is judged according to it; if it agree to it, well and good; it is accepted. If it deviate from the pattern it is thrown aside. A man rather prides himself on having concocted such a standard of value; it seems to him that it is a piece of originality; that it places him above other men; that he possesses judgment, discernment, tact, a discriminating mind.

He forgets that he has only taken another's model and labelled it his own. If a flock of sheep were passing a given spot and the first one jumped over an imaginary obstacle each of the others would do likewise. *So it is with men.* Here and there a member of the community breaks away from the rank, and then we term him a great man. It has been supposed that the number of such great men were limited, just as geniuses are, but as a matter of fact every human being is great. Every healthy mind has within untold possibilities, and the reason they have not evinced themselves is because their existence has never been suspected. For instance, possibly eighty persons out of every hundred who read these pages will smile in a superior sort of way when it is claimed that anybody can be rich who wishes. Why, they will exclaim, to amass wealth requires *brains, ability, cleverness,* and these are all wanting in the bulk of people. Quite true. These qualities are essential, but one is not justified in assuming they are the prerogative of the few.

Read the *biographies* of our merchant princes, of financial magnates of the world—your newspapers give you such cases almost daily—and note that they did not stand out brilliantly among their fellows at school. Some were among the densest, the dullest of their forms. In most cases no evidence of their being different from the common garden man was apparent for some years later. They simply had not *"discovered"* themselves, they did not know the stuff they were made of:

In the majority of examples they unconsciously stumbled upon forces which eventuated in their success.

Today, thanks to the new science of practical metaphysics, *man knows that he can attain the highest goal he can intelligently conceive,* and this through the medium of constructive thinking. Try to grasp this assertion. Think of the countless suicides which could be averted by such a belief, the immense happiness which could be brought to thousands of lives by its acceptance.

The fault with most people is that they *do not trust themselves.* They will seek advice from persons quite incapable of helping them instead of relying on their own interior powers.

To begin this constructive thinking try and find just where you stand. Take stock of yourself, mentally. Analyze your leanings, your tastes, the bend or trend of your mind. Do this only when you are in a normal state of mind—not when worried, angry, or nervous. No doubt several trials will be necessary to determine your line. Possibly you have been pursuing the right track but the wrong method. Alter the method. Take a successful man and note where he differs from you: in most cases it is executive ability. *Well, you can gain that. He* did not know the *Law, you* do, and hence you can do it more efficiently than he. Do you know your business from A to Z? Have you gone in for the latest or most up-to-date plant; do you pack your goods in the most approved fashion? Some countries have lost millions of dollars annually from bad packing, *Germany* scoring in this instance. Have you learned to hustle—not bustle? Have you overhauled your staff—assuming you have one? Are they reliable, capable? Have you all the details of the business at your finger ends? *Do you personally supervise it or leave it to a third-rate man?* Are you polite to customers? Do you organize a *"trouble department,"* placing a tactful man in charge who investigates all complaints, legitimate or otherwise, and settles the matter with the dissatisfied ones? These questions could be indefinitely increased— many will suggest themselves to you once you put your *thinking* cap on. It is then that you can determine if you are cut out for the calling you are now in, or if you could do better in some other line. Let your natural inclination have a hand in the debate with yourself, and you are not likely to get far out.

If you should find on going carefully into the matter that

you would have more scope in something which was more congenial remember it is never too late to change. Many of the most successful men in the business world today have followed callings very different from those to which they were brought up. Of course, one would not go to the other extreme, and attempt half-a-dozen lines at the same time. This has been a potent cause of failure, because the energies become scattered. Ideas which would bring to perfection the line on which a man chiefly depends are never realized, because before they are fully hatched they are tucked away in the mind to make way for some other problem which presses for solution at the moment, and afterwards the half-evolved idea either becomes forgotten, or the mind refuses to supply the missing threads which would make it perfect.

The importance of taking a real, live interest in one's work, whatever it be, has already been emphasized, and looked at in conjunction with the above it will be seen more clearly how success can be won.

Receptivity is not a frame of mind the average mortal cultivates; especially if he be a business man. He will tell you he has something better to do with his spare moments; that he barely has time to get through his work. *Yet the cultivation of receptivity is an absolute necessity.* It will be by freeing the mind of all worries, all plans, endeavoring to make it a blank for the time being that the most illuminative thoughts will strike—a literal, not merely a figurative expression—the mind. Where this frame of mind cannot be attained it will be found a good method to desire on retiring for the night that the answer to some question which demands attention should occur to you the next morning. Nearly always the subjective side of the mind, or the subconsciousness, will supply the information desired, and with a little more practice receptivity, which it must be remembered is the reverse of thinking, will be acquired. Then it is that you will find out whether you are on the right track in regard to your occupation.

Receptivity permits the entrance of thoughts which have long been struggling to express themselves in the ordinary consciousness. *Dickens* and other writers have put it on record how their *characters, conversations, incidents, and ideas* concerning their books leaped to their minds when in this mood —whence they could not tell, but modern psychology has, experimentally, demonstrated the source, analyzed the mechanism of the mind, and now can not only direct many of the operations, but can absolutely *create* any state of mind desired.

Run straight. When you indulge in sharp practices it is not the other fellow on whom you inflict the wrong, *but yourself.* It is the law that two thoughts of an utterly diverse nature can not occupy the consciousness at the same time. So long as you harbor a thought unworthy of an honest man you polarize your power of attracting, whether it be friends or money. *You can cheat others; yourself, never,* and he who essays to do so will sink back to the level of the crowd. Riches may, and often are, attained by unworthy means, but the man is the poorer, *for the Law is absolutely just.* There is no room in the universe for luck, for its existence predicates absence of law, to say nothing of injustice, and law is universal. A man who knows his inner forces, who expands his consciousness, who gains riches because as a part of the whole he is entitled to them, is oblivious to competition. He takes from the great storehouse of Nature, and no one is the poorer, rather by his efforts are others helped. To take advantage of a fellow creature, to grind and wring the uttermost farthing from a human being is to foul one's higher nature. For every cause there must be an effect, and like causes produce like effects, whatever be the plan, physical or moral.

One cannot handle pitch without being defiled, and ever to doubt the honesty of others is to *weaken* your own honesty. This is one reason why in this suspicious, critical age there is such a dearth of real happiness. To feel mean, angry, suspicious, is to invite those very qualities into your own being, to take their lodgment there and to undermine the character, and the man without character can never be truly rich.

There are plenty of cases of miserable wealthy people who would envy the happiness of poor men, so far as money is concerned.

Every human being is his *own nemesis,* from whom there is no escape, and it is about time this *law were known* and much unnecessary misery saved thereby.

It is as well to know something of the *law,* so that the weak-kneed may think twice before going astray.

Many people are in indifferent circumstances because they have never supposed they would ever be otherwise. They have expected it to be natural that some folk—the favored few—

should be wealthy, and others—the masses, with whom they identify themselves, should be poor. Hence they have not looked into their own natures to bring to the surface all the riches lying there.

Character is only another name for a set of ideas which have become crystallized, therefore we see people who are colorless because the life-thought which should be pulsing through their being can not flow on account of the condition of the channels, which have never been kept open since childhood. In childhood one's fancy is elastic, and one thing can be believed as easily as another. *Romance and imagination* die away with the years of maturity, and in place of the spontaneity of youth there grow sets of ideas, the product of the senses, the result of ready-made thoughts. Opulence, luxury, freedom from care, abounding health, get to be looked upon as the prerogatives of specially-selected individuals. Living among commonplace people tends to set the stamp of commonplaceness upon one, and the way in which this spreads is seen (in one direction) by the slovenliness of speech which is so conspicuous, and the equal slovenliness of newspaper English. There has always existed a dead level, though each generation raises it higher, and the active propagation of one-eyed ideas, which are driven into the minds of the people by a power which the past knew not—the *"hardtimes"* advocate—is more thorough than it used to be.

The low standard of the marriage state is another sign of the times, and the *passing of chivalry* and romance, which is everywhere apparent, is a still further outcome of them. The connection between all this and *Art of Getting Rich* is the decadence or the failure to use the idealizing faculties which cuts one off from an important source of wealth because one cannot readily *differentiate* oneself from one's environment.

It can be done, however, only the task may require more effort on the part of the man. The mental stagnation which strangles all clear thinking effectually shuts out ideas which would be money-making, and hides man's true greatness from him. The antidote is clear; another set of ideas must be substituted, and here romance may be reinstated. Practical dreaming is as good a term to employ as any. Build air-castles to your heart's content, but unlike the mere dreamer do not regard your creations as mere dreams. The more frequently you go over the picture the more clearly will the details stand out.

Where gaps were seen in the early attempts suggestions for filling them will occur; until at length the entire structure will stand out in the mind's eye boldly and perfectly.

The bringing down of theory to practice will simply be a matter of time, for the power which has brought into existence the abstract creation has merely to be extended to the concrete one now.

One immense step will have been achieved by castle-building. You will know what to aim at. Leaving out of consideration the masses of the cities there are millions of human beings who drift all their lives.

Want of purpose, want of objective, indifference, are the chief characteristics of this class, who will do anything but *think.* Tenacity of purpose, earnestness, bulldog determination, patient persistence never characterize these people.

As has been said, there is no magic about the method here presented; it is the working out of *unerring Law,* so that the man who lives the strenuous life, full of hope, *full of faith in his own inherent greatness, cannot fail to become rich.* The outcome of such lines being followed is the creation of an inexhaustible storage-battery, always charged, which can always be depended upon.

As the man progresses, as success after success results from his efforts he becomes filled with a *certainty* that all causes must be followed by effects. Even his mistakes—for he will make these for a time—will teach him lessons which before he failed to understand.

That marvellous, but little understood asset of the human make-up, the *intuition,* will solve problems as they arise, if the right *mental attitude is taken.*

This attitude is the quiet turning of the mind in upon itself, shutting out the without so that the voice of the within may be heard. Many a successful business man of today owes his success to the *flashes of the ocean of consciousness* behind the ordinary work-a-day world, and the power to let it *"come through"* can be attained by anyone.

All questions as to choice of calling, system, industry, thrift, investment, and the usual list of qualifications usually given to the aspirant for wealth, are in reality very minor, and need not be treated here.

TO RECAPITULATE.

It is now only necessary to *recapitulate* or cast into a concise form the propositions laid down in this *chapter*. They might be stated in these terms:

First—*Both the world and man are in their babyhood.*

Second—*The purpose of life is to express more life.*

Third—*More life can only be expressed by man's desires being fulfilled.*

Fourth—*Every desire must inevitably materialize, unless neutralized by a counter-desire.*

Fifth—*Science has not yet found any limits to the power of man.*

Sixth—*The capacity for more power comes with the fullest use of present capacities.*

Seventh—*The only obstacle which can prevent man from entering into riches or anything else he wants is doubt of himself.*

Burn these statements into your brain. Concentrate your mind upon them, whether in tram car, train, or walking, and fortify yourself by building up a strong inward confidence now and then, as opportunity offers.

There is no need to devote hours per day; it is the persistency which tells, and by cutting off the supply of pessimistic thought as served up for your delectation in the press, pulpit, conversation, pictures, and literature, and seclude your thought atmosphere for a time you will be the better for it.

To define riches is no light matter. Tastes differ and opinions vary. The *Vicar* of *Wakefield* was passing rich on £40 ($194.80) a year, but an individual with a large establishment and a high social position to uphold might consider $100,-000 scarcely adequate.

The writer would prefer to term that man rich who had sufficient to meet all his wants, which might be few or many, simple, or extravagant.

More effort would be required in the case of building up a big fortune than a modest competency, but the same principle would apply in each case.

The preceding pages are written in the midst of a *busy life,* and no pretence to literary style is made. The sole object in view the writer has kept before him has been to aid that ever-increasing class who, in a world of plenty, have not sufficient to gratify natural wants.

As to the moral side of the question the author contends that it is a duty every man owes to his country to have enough to keep him from want. By so doing he makes one pauper the less, and is in a position to help his fellows, for no man can truly rise without raising his fellows.

The new industries which have sprung into existence during the past two centuries, many initiated by single individuals, have found employment, some of it highly paid, to hundreds of thousands of people, in spite of what has been said of machinery ousting men.

Poverty has had its day as an *idyllic conception.* The world has had enough of it, and there are now other factors which will develop character in a much more satisfactory manner. Let those who still sing the praise of being poverty-stricken look the facts full in the face, and they will be almost bound to admit that in nearly every case it *dwarfs the man, crippling his finest feelings, and stunting his higher nature.*

Poverty is a crime—a crime against the state, and it is also as much a disease as any physical malady, and as such is curable.

The writer boldly asserts that no man or woman who applies the rules for getting rich can help becoming so; and the teachings can only be proved by being *put to the test.*

Reading is of little use. The pages *must be read and re-read* till they permeate one's being. No statement has been made which has not been demonstrated. If the student fails to demonstrate the truth of the assertions it is not they which are at fault, but himself. He is manipulating unchanging law, and his inability to demonstrate it is no proof of its non-existence.

FAITH IN SELF—BELIEF IN CHANCE.

"Faith in self is the—Key to Success."
"Doubt of self is the—Cause of failure."

Belief in chance is something, but *faith in self* is everything.

Belief in chance is sober, serious, grave, and respectable; *belief in self* is all that, and more too.

It is not second sight, nor is it the sixth sense, but it is *the life* of all of these things.

Faith in self gives one the *keen eye*, the *quick ear*, and the *business spirit*; it is the *interpreter* of all mysteries, the *surmounter* of all difficulties, the *remover* of all obstacles.

It is useful in all places, and at all times; it is *useful* in meditation, for it shows a man *his way* in the world; it is *useful* in business, for it shows him his way *through* the world.

Belief in chance may be power, but *faith in self is skill.*

Belief in luck, and chance, may have weight, *but faith in self is momentum;* belief in chance thinks it knows what to do, while *faith in self* knows how to do it.

Belief in chance makes a man respectable, *faith in self makes him respected;* belief in chance is wealth, *faith in self* is ready money.

For all practical purposes of life, *faith in self* carries it against belief in chance, *one hundred to one.*

Take them upon the stage of life, and put belief in chance *against faith in self,* and belief in chance will play a tragedy that will scarcely survive long enough to be hissed, while *faith in self keeps the house in a roar,* night after night, with its successful acts.

There is no want for dramatic talent which believes in chance; *there is* demand for dramatic talent *which has faith in self.*

Take belief in chance, and faith in self, before the bar of justice, and let them shake their learned fingers at each other's nose in legal rivalry.

Belief in chance sees its way clearly, but *faith in self is first* at its journey's end.

Belief in chance has many a compliment from the crowd, but *faith in self* receives the *fees* from its clients.

Belief in chance speaks loud and learnedly, *faith in self* logically and triumphantly.

Belief in chance makes men wonder that it gets on no faster, *faith in self* excites astonishment that it gets on so fast.

And the great secret is that *faith in self* has no weight to carry; it makes no false steps; it hits the right nail on the head; it loses no time; it takes all hints; and, by keeping its eye on the weather-cock, *is ready* to take advantage of every wind that blows.

Take them on the lecture platform.

Belief in chance has nothing worth hearing, *faith in self* is sure of an abundance of hearers; belief in chance may obtain a living, *faith in self will make one;* belief in chance gets a good name, *faith in self* a great one; belief in chance argues, *faith in self converts;* belief in chance is an honor to the profession, *faith in self* gains great honors from it.

Take them in business life. Belief in chance feels its way, *faith in self* marches promptly forward; belief in chance is ignored, *faith in self is obeyed;* belief in chance is sometimes honored with approbation, while *faith in self* is always blessed by preferment.

Take them in the *United States Senate.* Belief in chance has the ear of the senators, but *faith in self* wins their hearts, and *gets* their votes; belief in chance is unfitted for skilled employment, but *faith in self* fitted for it.

Faith in self has a knack of slipping *into a well-paying position* with as sweet a silence and glibness of movement as a billiard-ball insinuates itself into the pocket.

Faith in self seems to know everything, without learning anything.

It has served an *invisible and extemporary* apprenticeship; it wants no drilling; it never ranks in the awkward squad; it has no left hand, no deaf ear, no blind or lame side.

It puts on no looks of wondrous wisdom, it has no air of profundity, but plays with the details of place as *dexterously as a well-trained hand flourishes over the ivory keys of the piano-forte.*

Faith in self has all the air of commonplace, and all the force and power of genius.

GENERALIZATIONS FROM OBSERVATION.

If a man *possess* great talents, *he need not publish them;* they will generally publish themselves.

The love of knowledge *inspires an interest* in all humanity.

Speak after the manner of a *self-confident* man, if you would that all true men *hear and give you credence.*

Our best opinions and thoughts *are the strong ones.*

Selfishness and doubt are the fruits of a weak mind.

Faith and belief, in one's self, are the *symbols* of success.

Fill thy mind with useful knowledge, and *thou shalt avoid* empty words.

He who talks more than his share of the time *always* shows weakness and egotism.

The disappointed efforts of mankind in every department of life generally *originate and terminate in* secret selfishness.

Instead of enjoying life those who are destitute of self-confidence *live a compound funeral all their days.*

Sometimes the faces of those who have suffered while living *from a terrible doubt of self* are, for the first time peaceful when they are laid in the grave.

Often when men speak loudest their inward courage is *weakest.*

Honesty, faith and self-reliance are the three sparkling gems in the crown of *true* manhood.

Good ideas often take wings and fly *beyond our reach,* while bad ones cling to us like barnacles to a vessel.

True reason *ripens not* in the torrid zone of passion nor amid the frosts of bigotry, which always congeal truth.

The higher, nobler thought *was never dishonest;* therefore the divorced *were never truly married.*

Evil becomes supreme monarch of the mind *when seated* on the throne of a *selfish* ambition.

The exercise of *faith in yourself for health and good common sense* are the *best remedies* known to prolong human life.

Calm reason never seeks to prevail by unreasonable arguments.

The mind of the truly good changes often; *the heart never.*

A selfish man *covets that which he does not need,* while a liberal man often *bestows on others that which he really needs.*

Many men unwittingly enter into copartnership with error and doubt to *work out their own destruction.*

Many men talk as easily as they breathe, and with quite *as little* thought.

Meditation in the *quiet calm of nature* is the poising of the mind's wings for flight.

Men fail, sicken and die, through feebleness of will.

All the potencies of man reside in the will.

Practicability, from a material standpoint, congeals the fairest blossoms of mental flowers.

It is the small-minded, weak man who *quenches* the fire of his own success by his doubts and skepticisms.

To avoid obsession by doubt keep the mind positive and the body strong.

Obsequiousness begets friends; *truth,* hatred.

Hippocrates said to his pupils: "The affliction suffered by the body, the Soul sees when we shut our eyes."

Search for good in everything, and, when found, speak of it at once to your friends and neighbors, that they may rejoice with you that it has been found.

Sordid desires are the creatures of indulgence that *enslave men* to habits of error and wrong.

The prevailing misery throughout the world consists in placing *too little value upon self*.

Genuine friendship will always subordinate self-will to the welfare of a friend.

If you treat a man like a brute, *he is justified in behaving like one toward you.*

Thoughts, like many persons, are often more valued for their dress and surroundings than for their true character.

Public opinion is but the mist arising from the great ocean of thought and anon descending, it may be, in quiet showers or furious storms.

Conventional politeness is often but the chalice in which time-servers are accustomed to *offer us the poison of hypocrisy.*

A man who is always ready with an answer *seldom gives* the best one.

He who is a disturber in his own affairs *will not prove a peacemaker* in those of his friends or neighbors.

A profoundly *calm, thoughtful person* may be often sad, but never lonely.

A true man may ignore the rules of modern society and the dictates of fashion, *and yet not always forfeit his claim to good common sense.*

Truth lies in a straight line, following which a man may always stand erect in the full dignity of his manhood; but falsehood and error ever take a zigzag, underground course, pursuing which he must *bend his better judgment, twist his higher conscience, and warp his manhood till he ceases to be a man.*

Self-praise, like a circle, ends where it begins.

Many persons *revolve around great centres,* while others turn only on very small pivots.

From every dilemma there is always *more than one way out.*

The largest trees have always been found in *uncultivated* soil.

Endeavor that your forethought be as *unbiased* and far-reaching *as your after-thought must be.*

A thought that *does not command* one's own respect and admiration very seldom *commands that of others.*

The human will, *with a silent concentration of thought,* has the same effect on man's *"opportunities"* as the *magnet's* action upon iron.

As iron is brought near the *magnet it is at once imbued* with a subtle principle, *capable of imparting it to other iron,* if brought within its immediate atmosphere, while it neither gains weight nor changes in appearance, yet we all know one of the most subtle *potencies* has entered into its substance.

All human bodies are charged with different degrees of *mental forces,* whose strength varies with the condition and health of the person.

Very much *if not all nervous prostration* is either overproduction or lack of this fluid to sustain polarity, the loss of which produces imperfect health.

We often best enjoy that which we least understand.

A man's character can always be read *by the comparisons he makes.*

There are thoughts that often intrude, not as beggars, but as true gift-bearers.

None can understand the true *value of self-control* better than they who appreciate its blessings.

In youth many often woo and wed habits and errors from which in after-life they *strive in vain to be divorced.*

When men cease to bend the knee to mammon and become free from great possessions, they are in a more natural state of being.

Human faculties are nature's moulds in which ideas are given form.

Imagination is the mind's retreat, *when left in silence.*

Mental growth is, step by step, like the filling of a barrel, drop by drop.

The human mind is *nature's keyboard,* on which her harmonies and discords are sounded by the touch of, thoughts controlled, and, thoughts uncontrolled.

A well cultivated mind *makes* always a kindly critic.

Inordinate self-esteem makes a balloon of a man's head; all the rest of him is simply the basket.

An unstable mind is like the *meteor* in the midnight sky; it shoots through space, without orbit or direction, leaving but a momentary reminder of its existence.

A considerate man's first impression *is more reliable* than a hasty man's deliberate judgment.

Man *wisely* thinks ten times as often as he wisely acts.

Some minds are like those auction rooms which *have nothing* but second-hand furniture to offer.

Disappointments in life are the result of exaggerated hopes.

Great blessings often disgust *unappreciative and discontented minds.*

As we place rare jewels in a deep setting to enhance their beauty, so Nature sets man's mind in dark surroundings, that it may better *try his faith.*

The more egotism and treachery *become dangerous to,* and frequently *undermine* the cause of, freedom of all nations, the more does personal, material interest guide the acts and endeavors of men.

The man who in our era *is penetrated by a higher idea* and nobler sentiment appears to some people as a designing rogue, a visionary madman, or an enthusiast.

Instead of *love to man,* which as a paramount duty should lie at the foundation of all intercourse with his fellow-man, *mistrust* has become the first condition of judgment in the world.

Add to your knowledge—*"faith in self."*

Nothing possesses greater magnetism than *simple truth* well spoken.

All men should be good judges of human nature, *since all are actors.*

Merited rebuke from an inferior *has a double sting.*

Calm hope *gives* real moral courage.

Make use of time if you value eternity. Yesterday *cannot* be recalled; tomorrow *cannot* be assured; today only *is yours,* which, if you procrastinate, *you lose—which loss is lost forever.*

There is no better way known to man for *securing* mental and moral integrity than to encourage those habits, those methods, and those pursuits which tend to establish truth.

The things that appear delight us, but make the things that appear not, *hard to believe,* for the things that appear not to the natural eye are hard to believe.

The things most apparent to men are the evil of things, but the *good is a secret,* or hid in the things that appear, for it hath neither form nor figure.

Of this be quite sure. All that is rightfully yours *will come to you* in its own good time. *So reads the law.* "*Everything comes to the Man who in Silence can Wait.*"

It is the bright *oil of hope* which makes life's machinery run smoothly, and the fruit which generally gives the most happiness ripens on the tree of our best ideality and higher love.

Many of man's ideals of today *will be realities* on some golden tomorrow.

Hope is the mainspring of human action; *Faith* seals our lease of immortality; *Charity* and *Love* give the passport to the Soul's inmost, true, and lasting happiness.

Among the noblest sentences uttered by the martyred *Lincoln* was this: "*With malice toward none and charity for all, I seek only the good of my countrymen.*"

> Cross against corselet, Love against Hatred,
> Peace-cry for war-cry, *Patience is powerful;*
> He that *o'ercometh* hath power o'er the nations.

Do not be carried away by anger. As it is written, "*He that falleth on this stone shall be broken.*"

Opposition to peace is strife.

The first act of a living babe *is to wail a cry of pain;* the first expression of a dead face *is a smile.*

Does the babe *unconsciously shrink from the life before it;* and the smile *foreshadow* the peace *following* a life of toil? If so, life is a priceless boon, and the problem will be solved in eternity.

He who is *tolerant* with the intolerant, *mild* with the fault-finders, *free* from passion among the passionate, has conquered himself, and can truly say he has obtained *Mental Discipline*.

Truth always repays with priceless gems, the brave hearts who suffer for her.

Mental enlightenment, or thought-light, is the *product* of a well balanced mind.

The most ignorant mind has some form of thought or it would not be susceptible to improvement; *neither* would it be liable to defects.

We all feel *"enlightened"* when we come sympathetically into contact with a *calm superior mind,* and a flow of new thoughts is the result.

The process of mental culture goes on ceaselessly, with the sincere student, and thus his volume of thought-force improves, till *he pass out* of the sphere of doubt in self into that of *faith in self*.

Then the element *alters* and becomes more *homogeneous*.

Nature has no secrets from *her true votaries*.

He who would become one of her true disciples must first plant the *"tree of faith in self"* within his own mind and *culture it in silence* and patience.

In time it will yield to him the *true knowledge* of *success* and *failure*.

Thrice blessed is he who with *a lamp of truth,* in union with nature, has a natural inclination to develop his mind power without being driven to it by suffering and affliction.

Each must *carve out* his own way through life. Man can make his very contradictions harmonize with his *calm, quiet mind*. Try always to get better and better control of your thoughts. Go up higher and higher, ever trying to advance mentally.

It is far better to *try and try,* even if one make blunders, than never to have tried at all. When one is not strong enough to weather the gale, one must bow like a reed before it, rising again after the storm is past, more dignified, more grand.

Guard your weaknesses from most men; they are often either unworthy of your confidence, or in their friendship are very apt to abuse it.

Learn to know all, but keep thyself unknown, has been wisdom handed down the ages. Let your confidence and belief in yourself rest only on the heights of success.

To struggle on against all the world is *always unpleasant,* even if you be a thousand times right.

Do not strive to *pull against* the whole community where you live.

In silence and calmness listen patiently and do not argue.

You have *your freedom of thought.*

Isolation is best.

Better never to have been great than, having been so, *then fall forever to be so no more.*

A star that sets will *rise* again tomorrow; a star that falls rises *no more* forever. Search diligently for truth, no matter what the world may say. Press on, the golden *Star of Self-Reliance* is on the heights with its dawning lights.

On every height is found repose.

There come, to those souls who have no *faith in themselves,* times when they become *heart sick and weary.*

Alas! how many men of mature years are held back by doubt and self-condemnation because *they do not,* and have never, understood *what it means to have faith in themselves.*

The very best part of many men and women *lies buried* beneath their own fears and doubts.

Misunderstood, their fears hold them *down* with chains *forged* of *doubt and unrest.*

To all such a *change is necessary;* in fact, for the usefulness of their life, *a change is imperative.*

As the student acquires knowledge, he must learn how it has been acquired, and he is made to feel that no fact is worth knowing *unless with it he knows the way to prove it.*

Earnest student, *dare to be wise.* In silence *pursue the path of wisdom,* regardless of the world or what it may say, or any obstacle which it may throw in your way.

Be wise and *you will not only govern your own destiny but show others the way.* And you will possess a mind foreshadowing the future. By your prudence and foresight you will be able to counteract that which more gross or *untrained minds* have suffered to pass as fate or destiny, whereby their faculties are confined to a narrow line of operation.

I have—in THE MASTER KEY—given you the *Duality* of your being and *Salient* force.

DR. L. W. DE LAURENCE.

This is the end of this publication.

Any remaining blank pages are for our book binding requirements and are blank on purpose.

To search thousands of interesting publications like this one, please remember to visit our website at:

http://www.kessinger.net

Printed in the United States
69881LV00006B/5